A Guide for Using

Dear Mr. Henshaw

in the Classroom

Based on the novel written by Beverly Cleary

*This guide written by **Angela Bean Bolton***

Teacher Created Materials, Inc.
6421 Industry Way
Westminster, CA 92683
www.teachercreated.com
©1995 Teacher Created Materials, Inc.
Reprinted, 2002
Made in U.S.A.
ISBN-1-55734-541-4

Illustrated by
Kelly McMahon

Edited by
Cathy Gilbert

Cover Art by
Agi Palinay

Table of Contents

Introduction

A good book can touch our lives like a good friend. Within its pages are words and characters that can inspire us to achieve our highest ideals. We can turn to it for companionship, recreation, comfort, and guidance. It can also give us a cherished story to hold in our hearts forever.

In Literature Units, great care has been taken to select books that are sure to become good friends!

Teachers who use this literature unit will find the following features to supplement their own valuable ideas.

- Sample Lesson Plans
- Pre-reading Activities
- Biographical Sketch
- Book Summary
- Vocabulary Lists and Suggested Vocabulary Ideas
- Lessons grouped for study with each section including:

  — *a quiz*

  — *a hands-on project*

  — *a cooperative learning activity*

  — *cross-curriculum connections*

  — *an extension into the reader's life*

- Post-reading Activities
- Book Report Ideas
- Research Ideas
- Culminating Activity
- Two Unit Test Options
- Bibliography
- Answer Key

We are confident that this will be a valuable addition to your planning, and we hope your students will increase the circle of "friends" they have in books!

Sample Lesson Plan

Each of the lessons suggested below can take from one to several days to complete.

Lesson 1

- Introduce and complete some or all of the pre-reading activities. (page 5)
- Read "About the Author" with your students. (page 6)
- Introduce the Section 1 vocabulary list. (page 8)

Lesson 2

- Read the letters May 12 - November 23. As you read, place the vocabulary words in the context of the story and discuss their meanings.
- Choose a vocabulary activity. (page 9)
- Have students label the given place for each longitude and latitude coordinate point on the California map. (page 11)
- Have students conduct a personal interview. (page 12)
- Discuss the parts of business letters, and have students complete the activity. (page 13)
- Begin Reading Response Journals. (page 14)
- Administer the Section 1 quiz. (page 10)
- Introduce the Section 2 vocabulary list. (page 8)

Lesson 3

- Read the letters November 24 - December 21.
- Choose a vocabulary activity. (page 9)
- Make quiches. (page 16)
- Math connection: Have students complete "Think It Through." (page 17)
- Have students make a new friend and fill in a Venn diagram. (page 18)
- Administer the Section 2 quiz. (page 15)
- Introduce the Section 3 vocabulary list. (page 8)

Lesson 4

- Read the letters December 22 - January 31.
- Choose a vocabulary activity. (page 9)
- Have students write poetry relating to the book. (page 20)
- Design a postcard to Leigh's Dad. (page 21)
- Administer the Section 3 quiz. (page 19)
- Introduce the Section 4 vocabulary list. (page 8)

Lesson 5

- Read the letters February 2 - February 6.
- Choose a vocabulary activity. (page 9)
- Discuss interdependence of states for goods. (page 23)
- Graph amount of goods per state. (page 24)
- Discuss the book in terms of geography. Have students complete "Traveling Across the U.S." (page 25)

- Have students match feelings to graphics. (page 26)
- Administer the Section 4 quiz. (page 22)
- Introduce the Section 5 vocabulary list. (page 8)

Lesson 6

- Read the letters February 7 - March 15.
- Choose a vocabulary activity. (page 9)
- Discuss the book in terms of science - conduct magnetism experiments. (page 28)
- Perform choral reading "Inventions". (pages 29-30)
- Create symmetrical monarch butterflies. (page 31)
- Determine the cost of hardware store materials - math connections. (page 32)
- Assign either independent research investigations or book publishing projects. (pages 40-41)
- Administer the Section 5 quiz. (page 27)
- Introduce the Section 6 vocabulary list. (page 8)

Lesson 7

- Read the letters March 16 - March 31.
- Choose a vocabulary activity. (page 9)
- Discuss the book in terms of science - conduct electricity experiments. (pages 34-35)
- Discuss criteria for selected occasions. (page 36)
- Have students complete Parts of a Letter. (page 37)
- Administer the Section 6 quiz. (page 33)

Lesson 8

- Choose a vocabulary activity. (page 9)
- Reading Response Journals. (page 14)
- Discuss any questions your students may have about the story. (page 39)
- Begin work on the Culminating Activity. (pages 42-43)

Lesson 9

- Administer Unit Tests 1, and/or 2. (pages 44-45)
- Discuss the test answers and responses.
- Discuss the student's opinions and enjoyment of the book.
- Provide a list of related reading and quilt pattern for the students. (pages 46 and 38)

Lesson 10

- Finish the Culminating Activity.

Before the Book

Before the students begin reading *Dear Mr. Henshaw*, do some pre-reading activities to stimulate their interest in the book. The literature will be more meaningful when the students are given a solid background before reading.

1. Predict what the book might be about by looking at the cover.

2. Think about the title of the book and predict what it might be about.

3. Ask the children if they are familiar with Beverly Cleary. Set up a table display of Cleary's books and see which books they have read.

4. Ask if any students have kept a diary or read a book where the main character keeps a diary. Discuss the form and size of diaries and reasons for keeping them.

5. Have the students work in small groups to determine a list of helpful writing hints and/or a list of criteria used to judge stories in a writing contest.

6. Discuss the meaning of the Newbery Medal. Have students locate other Newbery Medal or Newbery Honor books. Share the following information about this award.

   Since 1922, the American Library Association has awarded the Newbery Medal to the most distinguished contribution to children's literature published the preceding year. The Newbery Medal was named for John Newbery, the first English publisher of books for children. One or more books are also named as "honor" books.

7. Ask students to think about the following questions and decide how they would respond to each of them.

   Have you ever:
   — felt alone?

   — been bothered by someone stealing from you?

   — kept a diary?

   — had an adult tell you he or she would do something that never occurred?

   — tried to write an imaginary story?

8. Use an atlas to locate a map that shows California, the setting of the story.

9. Choose another book by Beverly Cleary. (See the bibliography on page 46.) Make time each day to read aloud to your class from one of these books.

About the Author

Beverly Cleary was born on April 12, 1916 in McMinnville, Oregon. She received a B.A. degree in 1938 from the University of California at Berkeley and in 1939 a B.A. degree in librarianship from the University of Washington. In 1940 she married Clarence Cleary and became the mother of twins, Marianne and Malcolm. She worked as a librarian in the state of Washington and at the U.S. Army Hospital in Oakland, California.

Cleary remembers "We had no bright beckoning books with such words as 'fun,' 'adventure,' or 'horizon' to tempt us. Our primer looked grim." She grew critical, and asked, "Why couldn't authors write about the sort of boys and girls who lived on my block? Why couldn't authors write books in which something happened on every page? Why couldn't they make the stories funny?"

As a young child, Beverly Cleary discovered the pleasure and excitement of reading. Now she writes the stories that she wanted to read as a child. It is the "small daily ups and downs" that make these books such interesting reading for children.

Cleary's first book (written in 1950) was about 8-year-old Henry Huggins and his neighborhood friends, including Beezus and Ramona, who lived on Klickitat Street in Portland, Oregon. Cleary spent her school years in the farming community of Portland. She admits, "...As I wrote I discovered I had a collaborator, the child within myself...."

This author has written many, many books and has received numerous awards (at least 55) for her writing. Some of these honors include: the Laura Ingalls Wilder Award in 1975 for substantial and lasting contributions to children's literature; the Regina Medal in 1980 for continued distinguished contributions to children's literature; the American Book Award (for paperback) in 1982 for *Ramona and Her Mother*; and finally the Newbery Medal in 1984 for *Dear Mr. Henshaw*.

Mrs. Cleary's books range from picture books to stories for middle graders to novels for young teenagers. Her books appear in over ten countries in a variety of languages. Television programs based on Henry Huggins have appeared in Japan, Denmark, and Sweden. She has been a contributor of adult short stories to magazines, including *Woman's Day*.

The most difficult part of the writing process, admits Cleary, is "getting started, because it's very easy to put off. Once I get the first draft pinned down, the fun begins. Every book has a trouble spot though. When that happens, I've learned to put it out of my mind and turn to something else." Most rewarding about Cleary's career has been "the number of people who tell me of a child who didn't enjoy reading until my books came along."

(Information about Beverly Cleary was taken from *Something About the Author*, Volume 43.)

Dear Mr. Henshaw

by Beverly Cleary

(Dell, 1984)

(Canada, Doubleday Dell Seal; UK, Penguin, AUS, Transworld Publishers)

Dear Mr. Henshaw has received several honors. It was included on School Library Journal's list of "Best Books 1983" and the Horn Book honor list in 1983; received the Commonwealth Club of California Award, 1983; was selected by the *New York Times* as a Notable Book of the Year, 1983; received the Newbery Medal in 1985; and received the Christopher Award in 1984.

Leigh Botts first writes to Mr. Henshaw in the second grade, after his teacher has read Henshaw's *Ways to Amuse a Dog*. Leigh continues to write to the author in the third, fourth, fifth, and sixth grades. As part of a sixth grade assignment, Leigh sends a list of ten questions to Mr. Henshaw. Henshaw replies and sends Leigh a set of questions to answer also. Leigh's mother makes him respond to Mr. Henshaw's questions.

Leigh describes himself as "just a plain boy," probably the "mediumest boy" in his class. His dad is a truck driver, and his mother works part time for a catering business while she takes a couple of college classes. Leigh explains that his parents are divorced and that he really misses his dog, Bandit, who travels with his dad.

Leigh and his mother live near the coast in California. Leigh feels frustrated throughout the story because someone steals the good things from his lunch bag. Leigh often feels lonely, angry, and as if he is to blame for his parent's divorce.

Later, Leigh pretends to write letters to Mr. Henshaw in his personal diary. Mr. Fridley, the school janitor, tries to encourage Leigh and explains that Leigh is not the only child with problems. Finally, Leigh builds an alarm for his lunch box, becomes friends with Barry, and enters a story in the Young Writer's Yearbook. Leigh's alarm is successful, and his story wins Honorable Mention. He gets to go out to eat with a famous author who has met Boyd Henshaw. The author explains that Leigh's writing strength was that he wrote like himself and didn't try to write like someone else.

In the end, Leigh's dad returns to see if there is a chance for him and Bonnie (Leigh's mom) to get back together. By now, Leigh knows he can't count on anything his dad says. Leigh feels "sad and a whole lot better at the same time."

Vocabulary Lists

On this page are vocabulary lists which correspond to each sectional grouping of letters.

Section 1
May 12 - November 23

amuse	duplicated
diorama	gondolas
mobile home	enclosure

Section 2
November 24 - December 21

duplex	broker
bandanna	canapes
loner	quiche
cautious	partition
reefer	halyard

Section 3
December 22 - January 31

snitch	hibernated
fictitious	relieved
pseud. (pseudonym)	mimeograph
retainers	nuisance
tourists	wrath

Section 4
February 2 - February 6

herb	receiver
diesel	reception
mildew	sagebrush

Section 5
February 7 - March 15

antique	villains
eucalyptus trees	description
flitting	insulated wire
grove	hardware store
molest	demonstration
quivering	invention

Section 6
March 16 - March 30

prose	reserved
fad	garbanzo beans
tortillas	honorable
disconnect	forefingers
snoop	imitate
original	rejected

8

Vocabulary Activity Ideas

❑ Ask your students to create an **Illustrated Dictionary** of the vocabulary words. This could be an individual or group activity. Have students write the vocabulary words and draw a simple picture showing what each word means.

❑ People of all ages like to make and solve puzzles. Ask your students to make their own **Crossword Puzzles or Wordsearch Puzzles** using the vocabulary words from the story. Centimeter graph paper helps students make clear, organized puzzles.

❑ Play **Vocabulary Charades**. A small groups of students will compete as a team against another small group. A member from each team is given the same word to act out. The team that first announces the correct vocabulary word receives a point. A team's incorrect response causes them to lose a turn, and the actor must sit down. If no team guesses the word correctly, it may be used again later.

❑ Ask your students to **Write a Story** using at least ten of the vocabulary words appropriately. Encourage students to share their individual creations with the class.

❑ Challenge your students to create a chart or web to show how vocabulary words can be **Classified** under the headings: Nouns, Adjectives, Verbs, and Adverbs.

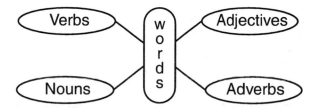

❑ Play **Vocabulary Concentration.** The goal of this game is to match vocabulary words with their definitions. Make two sets of cards the same size and color. On one set, write the vocabulary words, and on the second set, write the definitions. Groups of two to four students may play. Students mix all the cards together, and place them face down on a table. Students take turns picking two cards. If the cards match (the word with its definitions) the child keeps the pair of cards and takes another turn. The game continues until all matches have been made.

❑ Ask your students to **Collect Words** which are unfamiliar to them. Have students copy the sentence from the story in which the word appears, write what they think the word means, and check to see if their definition matches the definition in a dictionary. The form below may be helpful to give to students.

Word _____

Sentence _____

My definition _____

Dictionary definition _____

Page number _____

Quiz Time!

1. What does Leigh want to be when he grows up?_____

   _____

2. Name two books Mr. Henshaw has written._____

   _____

3. Why does Leigh get angry at Mr. Henshaw?_____

   _____

4. Why doesn't Leigh like his name?_____

   _____

5. What does Leigh's dad do for a living? _____

   _____

6. Describe Bill Bott's rig. _____

   _____

7. What does Leigh's mom do for a living?_____

   _____

8. How old was Leigh when he first wrote to Mr. Henshaw? How old is Leigh at the end of this
   reading section? _____

   _____

9. The following statements are events that happen in this section. Put a 1 next to the event that
   happens first, a 2 next to the event that happens next, and so on until all 6 events are numbered in
   the order in which they occur.

   _____Leigh starts answering questions from Mr. Henshaw.

   _____Leigh reads *Moose on Toast*.

   _____Leigh's teacher reads *Ways to Amuse a Dog*.

   _____Leigh gives a report on *Ways to Amuse a Dog*.

   _____Leigh sends a list of 10 questions to Mr. Henshaw.

   _____Leigh makes a diorama of the book *Ways to Amuse a Dog*.

10. What do you learn about Mr. Henshaw from his responses to Leigh's questions?_____

    _____

    _____

    _____

California Longitude and Latitude

In *Dear Mr. Henshaw*, Leigh Botts lives in California. His father is a trucker and drives across the state. Use a road atlas or encyclopedia to help you locate the following places on the map below. Then, place a dot on the California map in the proper place with the appropriate name.

1. Bakersfield—35 N, 118 W
2. Pacific Grove—36 N, 121 W
3. Taft—35 N, 119 W
4. Fresno—36 N, 119 W
5. Sacramento—38 N, 121 W
6. Death Valley National Monument —36 N, 116 W

7. San Francisco—37 N, 122 W
8. Yosemite—37 N, 122 W
9. San Bernadino—34 N, 117 W
10. Joshua Tree National Monument—33 N, 115 W
11. Los Angeles—34 N, 118 W
12. San Diego—33 N, 117 W

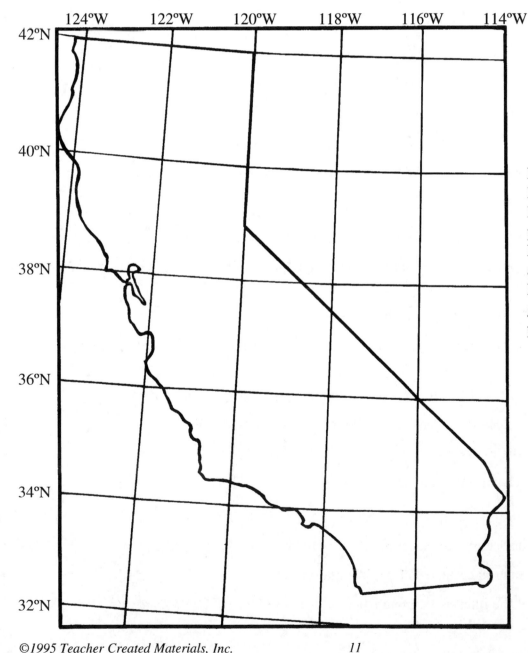

Lines of latitude and longitude are imaginary lines used to locate places on the earth. Latitude lines go east and west around the Earth. Longitude lines go north and south from pole to pole.

Personal Interview

One way to learn more about a person is to listen to the person answer questions. Leigh learns more about Mr. Henshaw by reading Mr. Henshaw's reply to his questions. Likewise, Leigh provides detailed information about himself when he responds to Mr. Henshaw's questions.

Working with a partner, conduct an interview to learn more about your classmate. Use the *Steps in the Interview Process* below to guide you with your interview. Put a check mark beside each step as you complete it. Be prepared to share the results from your interview.

You may also choose to interview someone in the school or your community for this activity. Consider talking to the principal, a janitor, a bus driver, a grocery store clerk, or a mail delivery person.

Steps in the Interview Process

Planning the Interview

❑ Brainstorm a list of questions to ask the person being interviewed.

❑ Write the questions on notecards, using one card for each question.

❑ Be sure the questions are open-ended, not yes or no questions.

❑ Organize the notecards so you can ask related questions together.

❑ Review the questions, making sure they will give the information you are seeking.

Conducting the Interview

❑ After a friendly greeting, explain the reason for the interview and begin asking the questions.

❑ Allow the person you are interviewing to answer each question fully before you ask another question.

❑ Ask follow-up questions about points that are not clear.

❑ If the answer to one question brings up another question that has not been written down, do not hesitate to ask it.

❑ Be polite and respectful of the answers and opinions of the person you are interviewing.

❑ Take notes on the notecards, or take notes and tape-record the interview.

❑ Limit the time for the interview.

❑ Thank the person for participating in the interview.

Sharing the Results

❑ Review the notes or listen to the tape recording of the interview.

❑ Organize the information collected during the interview.

❑ Share the results of the interview through an oral or written report, a newspaper article, or another tape of presentation.

Business Letters

On December 2, Leigh tells Mr. Henshaw that he is studying business letters. Business letters contain six parts: heading (your full address and the date), inside address (the company's address), greeting, body, closing, and signature. The letter could be a complaint letter, thank you letter, order letter, or application letter.

ACTIVITY

On the back of this page, write a letter to a company about a product you have recently bought. Describe the product fully and specifically. Remember to be polite and courteous. Refer to the sample below to use as a model for your own letter.

MODEL

1122 Main Street
Pacific Grove, California, 12347
February 2, 1995

Mr. Tran Smitter
Distance Electronics
2345 Circuit Drive
Bakersfield, California, 12236

Dear. Mr. Smitter:

A month ago I bought a 19" Supersonic color television set from you, model number 0300-B, serial number 1248-9223-88. All month the set has worked perfectly, but when I turned it on today, nothing happened. The trouble is not with the electrical outlet, which I checked by plugging in another appliance.

I would like you to examine the set here in my cottage, and either repair it free of charge or replace it with another 19" Supersonic. My telephone number is 689-8271, and you can call me any day from noon to 5:00 p.m.

Sincerely,

Bonnie Botts

Bonnie Botts

Reading Response Journals

One reason avid readers are drawn to literature is what it does for them on a personal level. They are intrigued with how it triggers their imaginations, what it makes them ponder, and how it makes them see and shape themselves. To assist your students in experiencing this for themselves, incorporate Reading Response Journals in your plans. In these journals, students can be encouraged to respond to the story in a number of ways. Here are a few ideas.

Provide the following response statements on a chart for the students. Tell them the purpose of the journal is to record their thoughts, ideas, observations, and questions as they read the book.

Response Statements

1. Write your feelings about what you read.

2. Write how you feel about a character.

3. Write what you think a character is like, compare characters, compare a character with yourself.

4. Make a prediction.

5. Compare to another story or event.

6. Illustrate a favorite scene.

7. Write about what you liked or disliked; always explain why.

8. Write about what you wish would happen.

9. Tell about something you feel the author should have included in the story.

10. Give your opinion of the illustrations.

11. How did you feel as you read? What do you notice about how you read?

12. Write any questions you have after reading.

- Provide students with, or ask them to suggest, topics from the story that may stimulate writing. One example from the letters in Section 4 is for students to rewrite *Alexander and the Terrible, Horrible, No Good, Very Bad Day* by Judith Voirst with events from the book about a terrible day that Leigh has.

- Ask students to draw their responses to certain events or characters in the story.

- Suggest to your students that they write "diary-type" responses to their reading by selecting a character other than Leigh and describing events from that character's point of view.

- Give students quotes from the novel and ask them to respond to each quote.

Quiz Time!

1. Describe where Leigh lives. _____

   _____

2. Why does Dad like to take Bandit in his truck?_____

   _____

3. How did Leigh get Bandit? _____

   _____

4. How did Bandit get his name? _____

   _____

5. Why doesn't Leigh have many friends?_____

   _____

6. Who is Mr. Fridley? Why does Leigh like him?_____

   _____

7. Name three things that bother Leigh. _____

   _____

8. What does Leigh wish? _____

   _____

9. When Leigh writes a book, what will he probably call it? _____

   _____

10. What does the California flag look like? Write a description and draw a picture in the box.

    _____

    _____

Cooking Time!

Leigh's mom works part time for Catering by Katy. Almost everyday, Katy gives Leigh's mom something good to put in his school lunch. She sends little cheesecakes, stuffed mushrooms, canapés, and sometimes a slice of quiche. Here are some recipes you can use to prepare a luncheon. As an extension bring in a favorite recipe from home. Be sure to include all ingredients that will be needed and specific directions to follow. Publish a class cookbook to share with families in your class.

Mini Quiches

1 package refrigerated pie crusts (2 crusts)

$\frac{1}{2}$ cup (110 mL) shredded Swiss cheese

$\frac{1}{3}$ cup (75 mL) mayonnaise

2 tablespoons (30 mL) half and half

2 eggs, beaten

2 tablespoons (30 mL) chopped green onion

$\frac{1}{2}$ teaspoon (2.5 mL) dry mustard

$\frac{1}{4}$ cup (60 mL) chopped ham

- Heat oven to 425° F (230° C).

- On lightly floured surface, roll each pie crust into a 12-inch (30 cm) circle.

- Cut each pie crust into twelve circles using a 2 $\frac{1}{2}$-inch (6 cm) biscuit cutter; place in lightly greased cups of miniature muffin pans.

- Prick bottom and sides with fork.

- Bake 10 minutes. Remove from oven. Reduce oven temperature to 350° F (180° C).

- Mix all remaining ingredients except ham until well blended. Spoon 1 tablespoon (15 mL) cheese mixture into each pastry-lined muffin cup; top evenly with ham.

- Bake 25 to 30 minutes or until golden brown. Immediately remove from pan.

Makes 24.

Salmon Canapés

1 (6 $\frac{1}{2}$-ounce) can salmon, drained and flaked

1 tablespoon (15 mL) low-calorie mayonnaise

1 tablespoon (15 mL) lemon juice

$\frac{1}{8}$ teaspoon ($\frac{1}{2}$ mL) dill weed

24 round crackers

6 slices cheese, any flavor, quartered

24 thin slices of cucumber

Parsley

- In small bowl, combine salmon, mayonnaise, lemon juice, and dill. Mix well.

- On each round cracker, place a piece of cheese, cucumber slice, 2 teaspoons salmon mixture and parsley. Serve immediately. Refrigerate leftovers.

Makes 24 appetizers.

Think It Through

In response to Mr. Henshaw's question "Where do you live?", Leigh lists several types of shops on his street.

Use the clues below to find where each store belongs on Leigh's street. There are two antique shops, a gas station, Taco King, Softee Freeze, a thrift shop, a pet shop, an electric shop, and a sewing machine shop. Arrange the buildings on the street according to the clues.

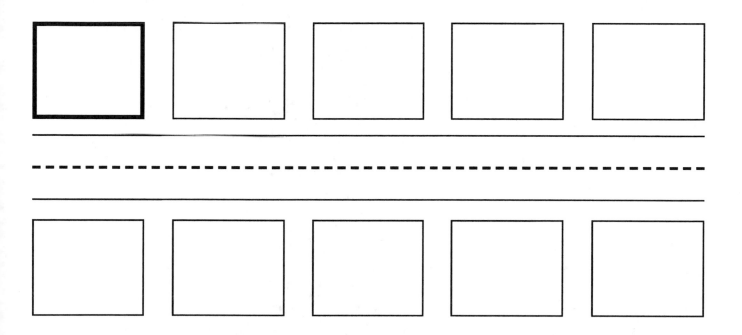

1. Leigh's house is outlined in bold.

2. The two Antique Shops are beside each other.

3. The Thrift Shop is between the Softee Freeze and the Electric Shop.

4. The Pet Shop is beside the Softee Freeze.

5. The Sewing Machine Shop is directly across the street from Leigh's house.

6. The Pet Shop is on the opposite side of the street from the Gas Station.

7. The Taco King is the last building on the same side of the street as Leigh's house.

8. The Gas Station is beside Leigh's house.

Make a New Friend

Leigh tells Mr. Henshaw that he doesn't have a lot of friends at his new school. He says that he has to be pretty cautious until he gets to know who's who. Have you ever had to go to a new school? It's not always easy to make new friends, but it's worth the effort.

Try making a new friend this week! First, choose someone that you would like to get to know, or have the teacher assign you a partner. Draw a Venn diagram on a large sheet of paper and use it as a tool to help the two of you get better acquainted. Label one circle for yourself and one for your friend. Let the circles overlap in the middle, as shown in the sample below. Put the characteristics that both of you share in the middle where the circles overlap. Put the ways in which you are different in your own portion of the circle.

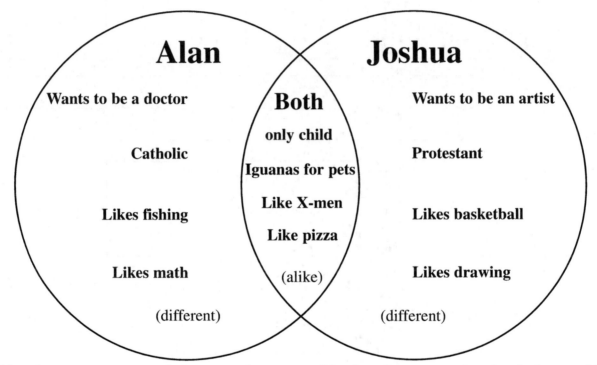

Finishing these statements can help you and your new friend get better acquainted and give you ideas of what to write in the Venn diagram.

My dream is to someday _____

My religion is _____

My family members include _____

In my free time I like to _____

If I had $10 I would buy _____

My favorite food is _____

One thing I like about school is _____

One thing I dislike about school is _____

My favorite TV show is _____

Quiz Time!

1. Why doesn't Leigh complain to the teacher about someone stealing the good stuff out of his lunch?

   _____

   _____

2. How does Bill Botts get a Christmas package delivered to Leigh?

   _____

   _____

3. Describe what Leigh's dad sends in the package.

   _____

   _____

4. What kinds of things does Leigh do during Christmas vacation?

   _____

   _____

5. How does Leigh fool the lunch thief?

   _____

   _____

6. Name two types of food that Leigh and his mom have for supper.

   _____

   _____

7. What does the school librarian have to give to Leigh?

   _____

   _____

8. Tell what the book *Beggar Bears* is about.

   _____

   _____

9. What is the prize for the writers of the best work for the Young Writer's Yearbook?

   _____

   _____

10. Why is Leigh sometimes left alone at night?

    _____

    _____

11. What problems may result from being a trucker?

    _____

Poetry Possibilities

Bill, Bonnie, and Leigh Botts make up songs (or poems) about lost shoes lying on the highway. Write one of each of the following types of poems using details from the story. You may write additional poems on the back of this page.

1. **Couplets** are two line stanzas that often rhyme.

   My friends all like to ride a bike,
   But I would rather take a hike.

   While hiking far from my abode,
   I saw a shoe upon the road.

   _____

   _____

2. **Triplets** are three line stanzas. All three lines rhyme in this triplet.

   I looked to see what I could see,
   While standing there beneath a tree.
   I jumped for joy to be so free.

   _____

   _____

   _____

3. **Rhyming Story Poems** often use a rhyme pattern of a-a-b-b-c-c, and so on to tell a story.

   High on a hill overlooking a stream,
   Elephant had an exciting dream.

   He dreamed of swimming like a fish,
   To swim the ocean was his wish.

   And so it was, one morning bright,
   He trudged downhill with all his might.

   That stream, he thought will get me there,
   I'll just jump in it, if I dare.

   _____

   _____

   _____

   _____

   _____

   _____

Design a Postcard

In the space below, design a postcard to send to Leigh's dad. Using the descriptions in the book, draw Leigh's street, Leigh's Christmas gift, the school, or catered foods from Leigh's lunch.

In the box below, write a message to Bill Botts from Leigh. Cut out the postcard and the message. Glue the message to the back of the postcard. Share the postcard with the class.

Quiz Time!

1. When do truckers have to pay a fine?

   _____

   _____

2. What does Leigh remember about traveling on the rig with his dad?

   _____

   _____

3. What advice does Leigh's dad give about the lunch thief?

   _____

   _____

4. How does Leigh feel while he talks to his dad on the phone? Explain why he feels that way.

   _____

   _____

5. Why does Leigh hang the phone up while speaking to his dad?

   _____

   _____

6. What does Leigh do while his mom has her women friends over?

   _____

   _____

7. Why doesn't Leigh scrub the mildew off the bathroom walls like he is supposed to?

   _____

   _____

8. Why does Leigh put a line through "Dear Mr. Henshaw" on Monday, February 5?

   _____

   _____

9. Why does Leigh's mom stop being in love with his dad?

   _____

   _____

10. What encouragement/advice does Mr. Fridley give Leigh?

   _____

   _____

Interdependence of States

Leigh's dad carries goods from one state to another. For instance, his dad drives along Highway 80 with a load of TV sets to deliver to a dealer in Denver.

For this activity, every student needs to bring in two wrappers or empty containers of grocery items. Then, students read the information on the packages and containers to find out where the products come from. On the USA map, students keep count of how many and what types of products come from each state.

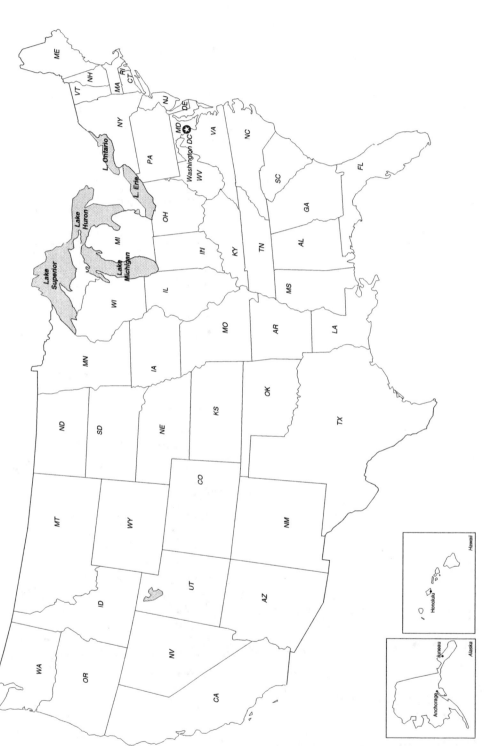

Interdependence of States *(cont.)*

Graph the Amount of Goods per State

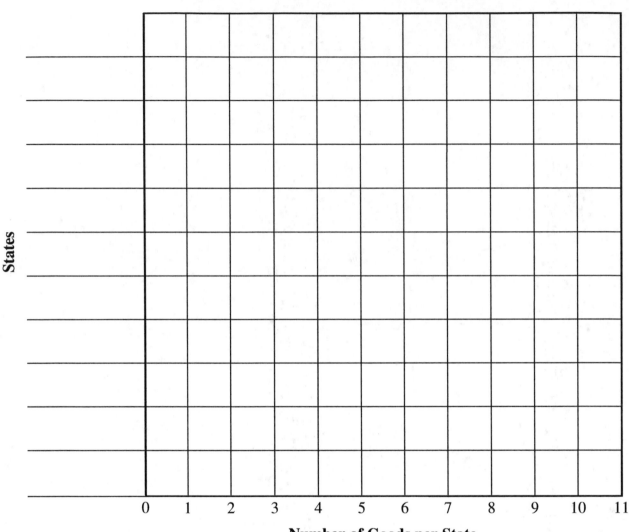

Number of Goods per State

Choose ten states. List the names of the states on the blanks down the side of the page. Color the correct number of boxes for each state to show how many products in the collection are from each state you chose. Then answer the following questions.

1. Which state made the most items?_____

2. What types of items came from your home state?_____

3. Which state(s) only had one product? _____

4. Which state(s) had more than three items? _____

Traveling Across the U.S.

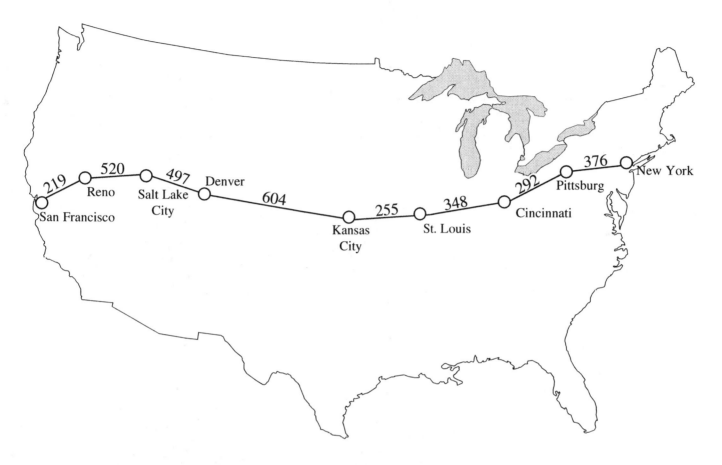

Leigh's dad takes broccoli from California to Ohio. On this map, we are traveling from San Francisco, California to New York, New York. Work with your group to solve these problems.

1. How many miles is it from St. Louis to New York? _____

2. How many miles is it from Denver to St. Louis? _____

3. How many miles is it from San Francisco to New York? _____

4. If you can travel 300 miles on a tank of gas, how many tanks of gas will it take to go from San Francisco to New York? _____

5. If you can only travel 300 miles on a tank of gas, where do you need to plan to make stops along the way to fill up your tank? _____

   _____

6. If you can travel 300 miles on a tank of gas, and a tank of gas costs you $15.00, how much will gas cost for the trip (San Francisco to New York)? _____

7. Some truck drivers do not stop for breaks along the way. Why would they do that? List any dangers you can think of in choosing not to stop. _____

* Information taken from *Mobile Road Atlas*, 1989

Feelings

Leigh reveals many of his joys and frustrations in his diary. Leigh explains that he is angry at his dad for losing Bandit and for taking another kid out for pizza.

Each picture below was designed to show a particular feeling. Match one feeling word to each picture. Write the name of the feeling on the line below the picture with which it matches. Be ready to give a reason to support your opinions. Meet in groups to discuss your answers. (There are no absolute answers to these exercises. Some common responses, however, appear in the answer key on page 48.)

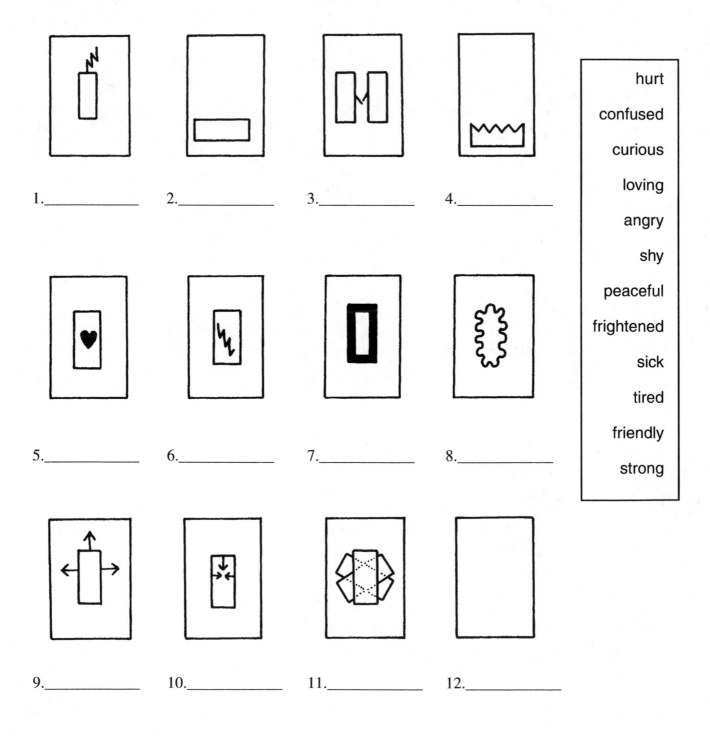

hurt

confused

curious

loving

angry

shy

peaceful

frightened

sick

tired

friendly

strong

1._____

2._____

3._____

4._____

5._____

6._____

7._____

8._____

9._____

10._____

11._____

12._____

Quiz Time!

1. Describe the place with the butterfly trees and tell how it makes Leigh feel. _____

_____

_____

2. What does Leigh notice near the roofs of some of the shops? _____

_____

3. What do boys in Leigh's class write about? What do the girls write about? _____

_____

4. What does Leigh's dad send to him from Albuquerque, New Mexico? _____

_____

5. What does Leigh plan to do with the gift?_____

_____

6. The following statements are events that happen in this section. Put a 1 next to the event that happens first, a 2 next to the event that happens next, and so on until all five events are numbered in the order in which they occur.

_____ Leigh gives his mom a demonstration.

_____ Leigh buys a beat-up black lunch box.

_____ From the library, Leigh checks out books about electricity.

_____ Leigh buys a light switch, battery, and doorbell at the hardware store.

_____ Leigh makes a "keep out" sign for his door.

7. What kind of lunchbox does Leigh buy? _____

_____

8. What happens that makes people notice Leigh at school?_____

_____

9. Describe the scene in the lunchroom when the alarm goes off._____

_____

_____

_____

Magnetism Experiments

Leigh does a lot of thinking and experimenting to rig up a burglar alarm. Since Leigh has never given much thought to batteries, he could benefit from conducting preliminary experiments about the forces of magnets. Work in groups of 3-4 students to complete these experiments.

What Do Magnets Attract?

You will need:

- two bar magnets
- a paper clip
- cloth

- nails
- paper
- an aluminum can

- a pencil
- keys
- a comb

- coins
- an eraser

Do this:

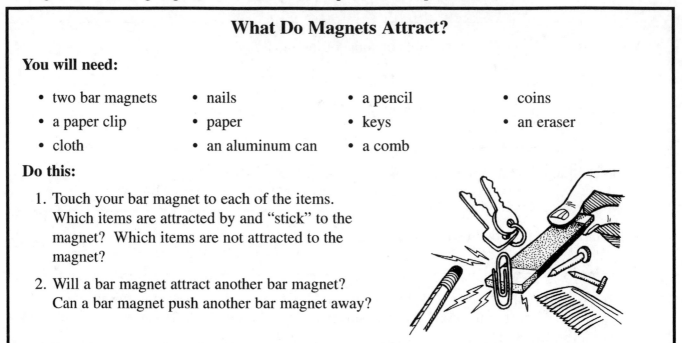

1. Touch your bar magnet to each of the items. Which items are attracted by and "stick" to the magnet? Which items are not attracted to the magnet?

2. Will a bar magnet attract another bar magnet? Can a bar magnet push another bar magnet away?

How Strong Are Magnets?

You will need:

- 3 magnets (horseshoe, disk, and bar)
- several sheets of cardboard (different thicknesses)
- tape

- several paper clips
- 4" (10 cm) piece of thread

Do this:

1. Slowly bring the paper clip close to each magnet. At a specific distance, each magnet will "pull" the clip. Can you feel any difference in the pull? Which magnet attracts at the greatest distance?

2. Now separate the paper clips from each magnet with a piece of cardboard. Does each magnet still attract the clip through the cardboard? Repeat this experiment using thicker pieces of cardboard (even wood). What happens?

3. Tie one end of a piece of thread to a paper clip. Secure the knot. Tape the other end of the thread to a table top. Slowly slide one end of the bar magnet toward the paper clip. Stop when you see the magnetic force begin to pull on the paper clip. Carefully lift the magnet, keeping it the same distance from the paper clip at all times. What happens? Will the magnet pull the paper clip through the air?

Choral Reading: "Inventions"

Leigh reads books from the library, gets tips from people, and invents a burglar alarm for his lunch box. Divide your class into groups to read this poem about historic inventions. As an extension have students complete a short research paper about one of the inventors mentioned in the poem.

Inventions might come by mistake,
     Like Goodyear whose rubber was dropped.
But often they come from hard work.
     And people who just can't be stopped.

Solutions are what they create.
     They ponder, test and re-test.
Ideas are put into use,
     Hence they've created their best.

There's Bell's fine ringing telephone,
     Edison's lighting our way,
And Robert Fulton's sleek steamboat
     Chug, chugging across the bay.

And ice cream makers for our homes,
     Nancy Johnson we should thank.
And 'cause the Wrights went flying high,
     Through clouds we soar and bank.

So when you spell America,
     Always dot the "I."
"I" is for inventors.
     That's the reason why.

Garret Morgan twice invented:
     Breathing mask and traffic light,
Lew Waterman, the fountain pen,
     So we could smoothly write.

And savvy Mary Anderson,
     To help us when it's wet,
Invented windshield wipers.
     How handy can you get?

From Madame C.J. Walker,
     For shiny, well-groomed hair,
A gift that made her our
     First lady millionaire.

The elevator Otis made
     Keeps moving on the scene.
In California Levi Strauss
     Invented the blue jean.

Choral Reading: "Inventions" *(cont.)*

So when you spell America,
      Always dot the "I"
"I" is for inventors,
      That's the reason why!

George Washington Carver, a slave
      At birth, with a mind that's free,
Found hundreds of uses for peanuts
      For you and also for me.

Typewriters gave us a boost,
      It's Latham Sholes we thank.
If not for Charles Kettering,
      Our cars would have a crank.

George Pullman made the sleeping car
      For railroad trips at night.
Mc Cormick's reaper reaps the rye,
      Much to our delight.

Potato chips are fun to crunch,
      George Crum created them.
And Hunt, he made the safety pin,
      Now you can pin your hem.

So when you spell America,
      Always dot the "I,"
"I" is for inventors,
      That's the reason why!

Fur trading for Mr. Birdseye,
      In Canadian cold,
Taught him how the Eskimos keep
      Their food from getting old.

The telegraph was made by Morse,
      The Colt Forty-Five by, yes, Colt
And Henry Ford's automobile
      Gave all the world a jolt.

You've heard some tales, but very few,
      There are so many more.
Inventors are a hardy lot,
      There's much more to explore.

Inventors have been rich and poor
      And many colors, too.
They're men and woman, boys and girls,
      They're people just like you!

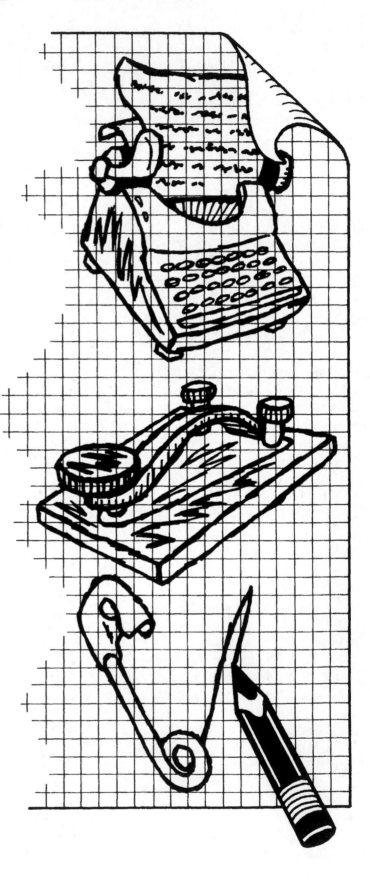

Symmetrical Monarch Butterflies

On Wednesday, February 7th, Leigh takes a walk after school. He happens upon a grove of butterfly trees and is surprised when he sees thousands of monarch butterflies float off through the trees in the sunshine.

1. Discuss symmetrical and asymmetrical objects. Symmetrical objects are the same on both sides. Let students give examples of each: body shapes, objects, and things that are easy to cut out of a folded sheet of paper.

2. Give every student one sheet of 9" X 12" (23 x 30 cm) black construction paper.

3. Guide students in folding the black paper in half with it laying horizontally.

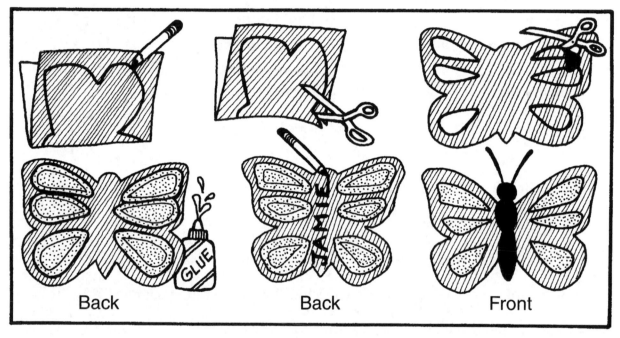

Back   Back   Front

4. Next, draw the shape of half a butterfly with the butterfly's abdomen being on the fold.

5. Begin cutting on the fold to cut out the butterfly. Students should keep their scrap pieces of construction paper to use later for main body parts.

6. After the butterfly shape is cut out, cut holes in the shape for colored tissue paper to show through. Encourage particular students to cut only a few larger holes, while others may choose to cut several detailed holes.

   Students should be careful when jabbing scissors through the construction paper, and they should leave good margins along the edges.

7. Now, students can choose tissue paper colors (orange for monarchs) to glue to the **back side** of the butterfly.

   Students should use only small dots of glue. It doesn't take much glue. Also, don't let tissue color overlap a hole, or the bright color will not show through. Excess tissue can be trimmed from the edges.

8. Next, students can write their names on the back sides of their butterflies.

9. Finally, a head, thorax, and abdomen may be cut from the left-over pieces of construction paper. Antennae may also be cut out. Then, carefully glue the parts to the set of butterfly wings.

Buying Hardware Supplies

Leigh takes his lunch box and twenty dollars to the hardware store. He buys a light switch, 6-volt lantern battery, cheap doorbell, and insulated wire.

The approximate cost for materials used to experiment with magnetism and electricity are listed. Use the prices given to answer the questions below. Remember to show your work.

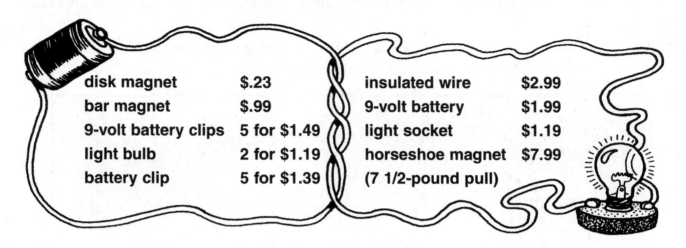

disk magnet	$.23	insulated wire	$2.99
bar magnet	$.99	9-volt battery	$1.99
9-volt battery clips	5 for $1.49	light socket	$1.19
light bulb	2 for $1.19	horseshoe magnet	$7.99
battery clip	5 for $1.39	(7 1/2-pound pull)	

1. How much will one 9V battery clip cost?

2. How much will one light bulb cost?

3. If you buy one magnet of each kind (disk, bar, and horseshoe), what will the total cost be?

4. Draw a picture of a complete circuit. How much will it cost to build your circuit?

5. You buy one of each of the items listed above. What is the total cost? How much change is left from the twenty dollars?

6. What is the difference in the cost of a . . .

    (A) bar magnet and disk magnet?

    (B) horseshoe magnet and insulated wire?

    (C) light bulb and socket?

7. Compare the prices of the two items below by placing <, >, or = in the box between them.

a battery clip   ☐   a disk magnet

Quiz Time!

1. Name the different topics Leigh starts to write about. Tell what he finally decides to write about.

   _____

   _____

2. Why does Barry have to disconnect his alarm?

   _____

   _____

3. What award does Leigh's story "A Day On Dad's Rig" win?

   _____

   _____

4. How is Leigh able to go out to eat with the Famous Author?

   _____

   _____

   _____

5. Why doesn't Leigh know what to say to Mrs. Angela Badger?

   _____

   _____

   _____

6. Why does Mrs. Badger like Leigh's story "A Day on Dad's Rig"?

   _____

   _____

   _____

7. What questions do the children ask Mrs. Badger?

   _____

   _____

8. What questions does Leigh ask Mrs. Badger? What is her reply?

   _____

   _____

9. Why is Leigh glad that he doesn't know who the thief is?

   _____

   _____

10. How does Leigh feel about his burglar alarm? Give proof from the story.

   _____

   _____

   _____

Electricity Experiments

Leigh learns about batteries, switches, and insulated wire when he builds a burglar alarm for his lunch box. You too can learn about electricity by conducting these experiments.

How to Strip Wire

(Stripping wire is removing the plastic covering from the wire's ends to allow you to connect it to other wires or hardware.)

You will need: • plastic-coated copper wire   • pair of scissors

Do this:

1. Using a blunt pair of scissors, make a small cut all around the plastic covering about one inch (2.5 cm) from the end of the wire. Be careful not to cut into the copper itself—just the plastic.
2. Grab the plastic covering. Gently twist and pull it off.
3. Practice until you can strip wire without damaging the copper inside.

Light Your Mini-Lamp

To have an electric current, a "circuit" is required. A circuit is a complete path that begins and ends at the same place. If the path is broken, the electricity will not flow.

You will need: • three 1' (30 cm) pieces of wire   • a 9-volt battery
                      • a light bulb and socket   • a battery clip

Do this:

If you think the light bulb will light, write *Yes* in the box. If you think it will not light, write *No*. Then, test the experiments.

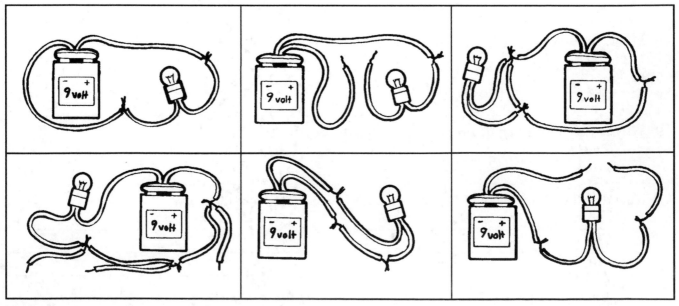

Electricity Experiments *(cont.)*

Insulator or Conductor?

Conductors provide an easy path for electricity to flow through. Insulators, on the other hand, make it impossible for electricity to flow through them.

Look at the chart. Read the list of items. Circle Yes if you think the object will conduct enough electricity to light the light bulb. If you don't think the light bulb will light, circle No. See if you can predict which materials are conductors and which are insulators. Then, construct a circuit test to check the objects and find out.

Material	Prediction	Did It Light?	Insulator or Conductor?
aluminum foil	Yes No	Yes No	
eraser	Yes No	Yes No	
coins	Yes No	Yes No	
key	Yes No	Yes No	
pencil	Yes No	Yes No	
rock	Yes No	Yes No	
paper clip	Yes No	Yes No	
plastic	Yes No	Yes No	

Materials:

- small bulb with wires
- 9 volt battery
- key
- pencil
- rock
- plastic
- aluminum foil
- eraser
- coins
- paper clip

Do this:

1. Connect one of the bulb wires to the wire leading from the battery.

2. While holding only the insulated parts of the wires, touch the object to be tested with the ends of the wires as shown. Do not let the wires touch each other.

3. Observe the bulb. Does it light? Record your results in the table. Write Insulator if the object is an insulator, or Conductor if it's a conductor.

Determining Criteria

Criteria are the standards on which a judgment is based. Leigh's story "A Day On Dad's Rig" is judged on a set of criteria established by the judges for the Young Writer's Yearbook. Leigh wins Honorable Mention.

As a group, decide on a list of criteria for each situation explained below. Make a chart for the class listing the criteria your group has decided upon for each situation.

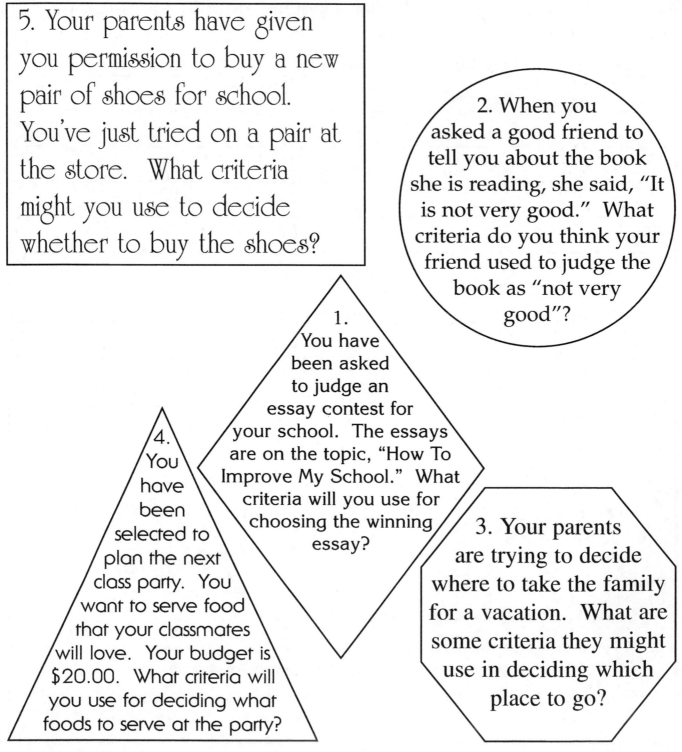

5. Your parents have given you permission to buy a new pair of shoes for school. You've just tried on a pair at the store. What criteria might you use to decide whether to buy the shoes?

2. When you asked a good friend to tell you about the book she is reading, she said, "It is not very good." What criteria do you think your friend used to judge the book as "not very good"?

1. You have been asked to judge an essay contest for your school. The essays are on the topic, "How To Improve My School." What criteria will you use for choosing the winning essay?

4. You have been selected to plan the next class party. You want to serve food that your classmates will love. Your budget is $20.00. What criteria will you use for deciding what foods to serve at the party?

3. Your parents are trying to decide where to take the family for a vacation. What are some criteria they might use in deciding which place to go?

Parts of a Letter

Leigh wrote a letter. He was proud that he had the correct letter parts, capitalization, and punctuation. But Leigh forgot one thing. The parts of a letter must be in the correct place on the page. On the back of this page, write Leigh's letter correctly. The parts of a letter are shown at the right.

	Heading
Greeting	
Body	
	Closing
	Signature

**February 6, 1995 Dear Bandit,
I hope I get to see you again. I wish
you were here to keep me company. I
wonder whether you are lost or whether you
jumped into another truck. I hope you are warm
and healthy! You kept Dad company on the long
hauls. I miss my dad, too. I wonder if
another boy has taken my place. Yours
truly, Leigh**

Now, answer these questions about writing letters.

1. What punctuation mark in a business letter is different from the punctuation in a friendly letter?

2. Which part of a business letter is not found in a friendly letter?

3. Name other phrases that would be good closings.

4. Where must commas be placed in a friendly letter?

5. What words in a friendly letter are always capitalized?

Challenge: Compare the business letter that you have written previously (page 13) to this friendly letter. How is a business letter different from a friendly letter?

Challenge: Draw a Venn diagram comparing a business letter to a friendly letter. Label one circle for business letter and one for friendly letter. Let the circles overlap in the middle. Put the characteristics that both types of letters share in the middle where the circles overlap.

Related Reading Quilt

As you read a book, color in the matching quilt section. Add the book title and a few lines of summary. When you have colored the entire quilt, it will be placed on display in our classroom.

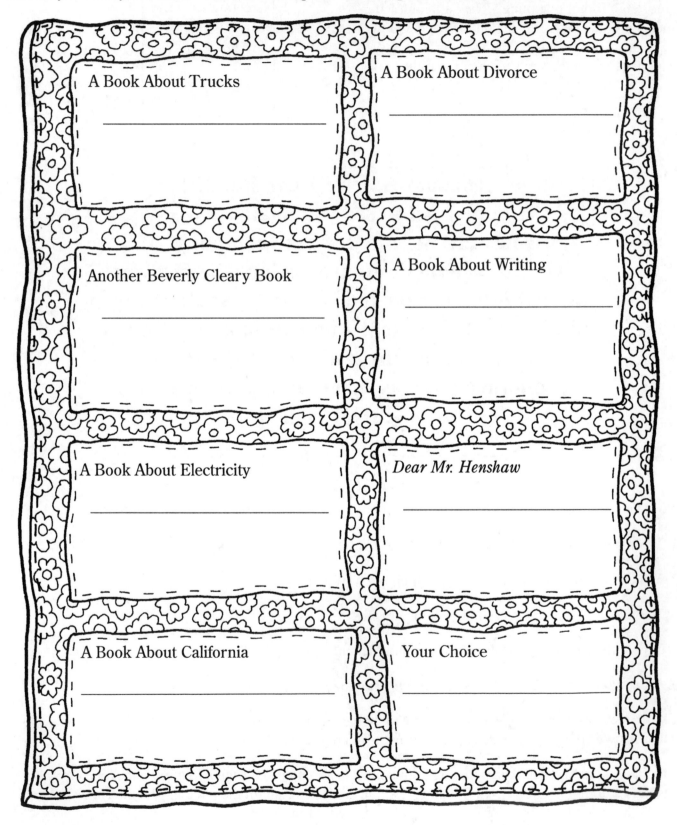

A Book About Trucks

_____

A Book About Divorce

_____

Another Beverly Cleary Book

_____

A Book About Writing

_____

A Book About Electricity

_____

Dear Mr. Henshaw

_____

A Book About California

_____

Your Choice

_____

Any Questions?

When you finished reading *Dear Mr. Henshaw*, did you have some questions that were left unanswered? Write some of your questions here.

_____

_____

_____

_____

Work in groups or by yourself to prepare possible answers for some or all of the questions you have asked above and those written below. When you have finished writing your predictions, share your ideas with the class.

- Does Bill Botts ever return to Pacific Grove to see Leigh? Does he see Leigh more often?

- What is Leigh's favorite subject in school? What is his school like?

- Does Bonnie Botts become a nurse? Does she move into another house?

- Does Leigh write a story next year for the Young Writer's Yearbook? Does he continue to keep a diary and write to Mr. Henshaw?

- Does anyone try to steal from Leigh's lunch again? Does Leigh become more popular at school?

- Does Leigh grow up to be a writer, librarian, electrician, or truck driver? Does Leigh go to college? Does he ever meet Mr. Henshaw?

- What would have happened if Leigh had never entered his story in the Young Writer's Yearbook?

- Does anyone find out who the thief is? What punishment does the thief receive?

- If Bill Botts was in a trucking accident and could no longer drive, would Bonnie get back together with him?

- Leigh's third grade teacher explains a trick about spelling "friend." List three or more spelling rules. What are the exceptions to the rules?

Book Report Ideas

- **Pretend to Interview the Author**

  Interview the "author" of your book about the characters she chose. Record your answers and questions on a tape recorder. Try to make your voice sound like two different people. Start out with this basic question: Who are the main characters?

  Then answer these questions about one of the main characters:

  What problem or difficulty did he face?

  How did he feel about his problems?

  How did he solve his problems? Who helped?

- **Design a Shoe Box Diorama or "Peephole Box"**

  Draw a background picture to paste into a shoe box. Then, add cardboard and/or three dimensional objects and characters to create a scene from the story. Be prepared to explain why you made certain choices for what is included in the scene.

- **Create a Mobile**

  Start by setting the scene at the top level, characters at the middle, and develop the plot at the bottom level. Be sure to put pictures on both sides.

- **Create a Book Jacket**

  On the front cover, write the title, author's name, and an illustration of the book. On the back cover, write a summary of the events in the book. Write your own name in the bottom right-hand corner. On the inside front flap, write a detailed description of the main character of the book. On the inside back flap, write down the reasons why you liked the book.

- **Draw a Poster to Advertise Your Book**

  Make it very detailed to show the setting, being sure to depict at least one character and one major event in the book. Be sure to include the title and author's name.

- **Create a Time-line Poster**

  Show the sequence of five or more main events that happen in Leigh's life. You may draw pictures of the events to represent photographs. Any time-line design is appropriate if it shows a definite sequence of the order in which the events occur in the story.

- **Present a One-person Show**

  Videotape your show. Become Leigh Botts and talk directly to the audience.

- **Draw a Comic Strip**

  Choose two characters from the book. Draw a four-frame comic strip about a real or imaginary conversation they have. Write their words in balloons.

- **Draw and Dream**

  Draw a picture about what you think the main character would like to dream about. Then describe the dream in writing. Would your dreams be like the main character's, or different? Write why.

Research Ideas

Describe three things you read in *Dear Mr. Henshaw* that you would like to learn more about.

1._____

2._____

3._____

Work in groups to research one or more of the areas you named above, or choose from the areas that are mentioned below. Share your findings with the class in any appropriate form of oral presentation.

- The Pacific States
- Thomas A. Edison
- Electricity
- State flags
- Monarch butterflies
- Types of poetry
- Careers
    - nursing
    - librarian
    - caterer
    - trucker
    - custodian
    - writer

- Major products from the states in the U.S.
- Ben Franklin and how electricity was discovered
- Other stories where characters keep a diary
- Favorite writing topics of students at your school
- Feeding animals in national parks
- Inventions/Inventors
- CB radios - their history and use
- Yellowstone National Park
- Highways and Interstates
- Newbery Medal Books
- Creative Cooking/Catering
- Kinds of homes
- Long distance phone call services

Character Development Matrix

As we follow Leigh Botts from second grade through sixth grade, he goes through several changes as a result of the events and experiences he encounters. This matrix will provide students with a visual way to analyze and explore how a character evolves. Students may rank Leigh's experiences differently, depending upon their personal experiences and beliefs. The main focus of the activity is to provide students with the opportunity to make decisions, give reasons for their choices, and to allow the teacher to hear how students think things through. Follow the steps below:

1. Have the students describe at least five to seven of Leigh's main experiences and explain how each event affects Leigh. The series of questions outlined below will help students analyze how the main character develops.
   A. What does Leigh do at the beginning of the story?
   B. What happens to Leigh next?
   C. Which event makes Leigh the angriest, the most surprised, the most hurt, and feel the best or happiest?
   D. What experience will Leigh remember most powerfully when he is ten years older?
   E. When does Leigh seem to act the most mature?
   F. What is the greatest consequence of one of Leigh's actions?

2. Next, divide students into small groups. Several groups of students will prepare a final copy of Leigh's main experiences and draw a matching illustration on a sheet of 8 ½" x 11" (22 x 28 cm) paper.

3. Other students may draw a grid on chart paper. The horizontal axis is labeled "Leigh's Experiences," and the vertical axis is labeled from one to ten with the zero point where the two axes meet.

4. Have children select the most significant experience in Leigh's life. Place that illustration in the correct sequence at the "ten" place on the vertical axis.

5. Once students have decided on the most powerful experience or event in Leigh's life, they can discuss and place the rest of the illustrations accordingly. A sample appears below:

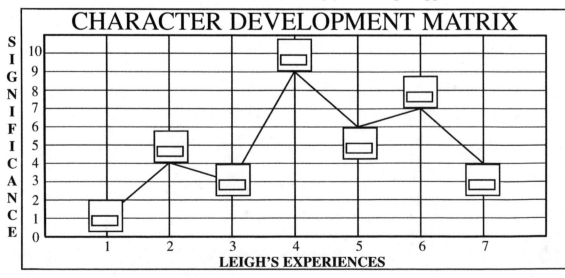

Extension: After the matrix has been made and discussed, students may reproduce the information on a sheet of paper in the form of a bar graph or pie graph. They may create the graph as they desire and make summarizing statements about the character.

News Interview

Leigh and Boyd Henshaw have planned to meet each other in a park in Bakersfield, California. A news reporter finds out about it. He decides that this will make a great human interest story for television. You may wish to provide a camcorder and possibly a microphone.

Have students work in small groups to conduct interviews. As a group, they can decide what answer a certain character will give. During the interview program, the group's members can assume the roles of newscaster, camera operator, Leigh, Mr. Henshaw, etc.

Interviewer: "Mr. Henshaw and Leigh Botts, thank you both for allowing me to be here, and for being willing to tell us about your story."

_____

_____

Interviewer: "How did you begin writing to each other?"

_____

_____

Interviewer: "Mr. Henshaw, why did you write such sarcastic answers back to Leigh when he needed to write a report about you for school?"

_____

_____

Interviewer: "Leigh, why did you feel so angry toward Mr. Henshaw?"

_____

_____

Interviewer: "Mr. Henshaw, what advice did you give to Leigh about writing?"

_____

_____

Interviewer: "Leigh, describe the situation when you went to lunch with author Angela Badger."

_____

_____

_____

Interviewer: "What caused you two to finally meet each other in person?"

_____

_____

Unit Test

Matching: Match each person with the words that best relate to him or her.

1._____ Leigh Botts   A. "Look out. Don't lose your false teeth."

2._____ Bill Botts   B. "I don't have kids because I don't raise goats."

3._____ principal   C. "I had to chain up on Highway 80 and lost time."

4._____ librarian   D. "Whenever I watch the waves, I feel that...life will still go on."

5._____ Mr. Henshaw   E. "I'm going to get whoever steals from my lunch."

6._____ Mr. Fridley   F. "That's quite an invention you have there."

7._____ Barry   G. "Have you written anything for the Young Writer's Yearbook?"

8._____ Bonnie Botts   H. "I would like an alarm like that on the door of my room at home."

True or False: Write true or false next to each statement below.

_____ 1. Beverly Cleary wrote letters to Mr. Henshaw.

_____ 2. Leigh gets to meet Mr. Henshaw.

_____ 3. Bandit freezes to death.

_____ 4. Leigh finds out who the lunch thief was.

_____ 5. Leigh gives the twenty dollars to his mom.

Short Answer: Provide a short answer to complete correctly each of these statements.

1._____ tells Leigh he needs a burglar alarm on his lunch bag.

2._____ becomes one of Leigh's friends and invites Leigh over to his house.

3._____ tells Leigh there should be a new paragraph when a different person speaks.

4._____ sends Leigh little cheesecakes, stuffed mushrooms, and canapes.

Essay: Write the answers to these questions on the back of this paper.

1. People are important to Leigh. Choose one character from the book. Explain why that person is important to Leigh.

2. Leigh loves Bandit very much. What thoughts might be going through Leigh's mind when he tells his dad to keep Bandit?

3. List three different authors whose books you have read in the last three to four years. Do you have a favorite on that list? Write a short paragraph about the books you have read by one of the three authors you have listed. Tell about the books, characters, and why you like the books. Give specific reasons why you like to read books by this author.

Response

Discuss the meaning of these quotations from *Dear Mr. Henshaw*. Identify who is speaking. Describe the circumstances or the setting. Comment on what meaning might have been intended beyond the exact words in the quote.

Note to the teacher: Choose an appropriate number of quotes to which your students should respond.

Section 1 (May 12 - November 23)

We licked it.

Please would you write to me in your own handwriting? I am a great enjoyer of your books.

I need your answer by next Friday. This is urgent!

Maybe I won't even read any more of your books.

I am sort of medium....I guess you could call me the mediumest boy in the class.

Section 2 (November 24 - December 21)

Mom says maybe I'm a loner, but I don't know.

I don't have a favorite teacher, but I really like Mr. Fridley.

I am bothered about walking to school slow.

Why can't he say he misses me, and why can't he call me Leigh?

The first page still looks the way I feel. Blank.

Section 3 (December 22 - January 31)

I can't complain to the teacher because it isn't a good idea for a new boy in school to be a snitch.

We're divorced. Remember? I remember all right. I remember all the time.

He sent a call over his CB radio for someone coming to Pacific Grove who would like to play Santa.

It takes two people to get a divorce.

Section 4 (February 2 - February 6)

Hey, Bill, Mom wants to know when we're going out to get the pizza?

I don't want to see a boy like you get into trouble, and that's where you're headed.

Section 5 (February 7 - March 15)

They made me think of a story Mom used to read me about Cinderella returning from the ball.

Here's $20. Go buy yourself an ice cream cone.

A character in a story should solve a problem or change in some way.

I began to feel like some sort of hero. Maybe I'm not so medium after all.

Section 6 (March 16 - March 31)

You wrote like you, and you did not try to imitate someone else.

On the ride home, everybody was chattering about Mrs. Badger. I didn't want to talk. I just wanted to think.

I felt sad and a whole lot better at the same time.

Bibliography

Aliki. *How a Book is Made.* (Harper Collins, 1988)

Ardley, Neil. *Discovering Electricity.* (Watts, 1984)

Aylesworth, Thomas and Virginia. *Let's Discover the States: The Pacific.* (Chelsea House, 1988)

Bains, Rae. *Discovering Electricity.* (Troll Associates, 1982)

Barrett, N.S. *Trucks.* (Watts, 1984)

Behrens, June. *I Can Be a Truck Driver.* (Children's Press, 1985)

Berry, Joy Wilt. *What To Do When Your Mom or Dad Says ... "Write to Grandma!"* (Children's Press, 1984)

Blume, Judy. *It's Not the End of the World.* (Bradbury, 1972)

Broekel, Ray. *Trucks.* (Children's Press, 1983)

Brown, Laurene. *Dinosaurs Divorce: A Guide for Changing Families.* (Atlantic, 1986)

Challand, Helen J. *Experiments With Electricity.* (Children's Press, 1986)

Cleary, Beverly. *Ramona Forever.* (Morrow, 1984)

  Ramona the Pest. 1968.

  Ramona the Brave. 1975.

  Ralph S. Mouse. 1984.

  Runaway Ralph. 1970.

  Henry and the Clubhouse. 1962.

  Henry and Ribsy. 1954.

  Beezus and Ramona. 1955.

  Socks. 1973.

  The Mouse and the Motorcycle. 1965.

  Sister of the Bride. 1963.

  Emily's Runaway Imagination. 1961.

  Ribsy. 1982.

Cooke, David. *How Books Are Made.* (Dodd, 1963)

Corbett, Scott. *The Mailbox Trick.* (Atlantic Monthly Press, 1961)

Fradin, Dennis. *California in Words and Pictures.* (Children's Press, 1977)

Freeman, Ira. *All About Electricity.* (Random, 1957)

Fritz, Jean. *What's the Big Idea Ben Franklin?* (Putman, 1982)

Geography of the U.S.: Pacific States. (National Geographic Society, 1979)

Great American Favorite Brand Name Cookbook. (Publications International, 1993)

Greene, Carol. *How A Book Is Made.* (Children's Press, 1988)

Jacobsen, Helen and Florence Mischel. *The First Book of Letter Writing.* (Watts, 1957)

Jefferis, David. *Giants of the Road: History of Land Transportation.* (Watts, 1991)

Jennings, Terry. *Electricity.* (Gloucester, 1990)

Johnston, Tom. *Electricity Turns The World On!* (G. Stevens, 1988)

Langley, Andrew. *Let's Look At Trucks.* (Bookwright Press, 1989)

Mobile Road Atlas and Trip Planning Guide. (Prentice Hall, 1989)

Retan, Walter. *The Big Book of Real Trucks.* (Grosset and Dunlap, 1987)

Rocco, Feravolo. *Junior Science Book of Electricity.* (Garrard, 1960)

Siebert, Diane. *Truck Song.* (Crowell, 1984)

Sobol, Harriet. *My Other-Mother, My Other-Father.* (Macmillan, 1979)

Answer Key

Page 10 - Section 1: Quiz Time!

1. A famous book writer with a beard like Mr. Henshaw.
2. *Ways to Amuse a Dog* and *Moose on Toast.*
3. Mr. Henshaw sends Leigh ten questions.
4. Some people don't know how to say it or think it is a girl's name.
5. He drives a big truck.
6. It's a cab-over job, with a bunk in the cab. It has ten wheels, two in front and eight in back.
7. She works part time for Catering by Kay. She also takes courses at the community college to become a Licensed Vocational Nurse.
8. Second grade. Sixth grade.
9. Order of events: 6, 4, 1, 3, 5, 2.
10. He gives silly answers and he is busy writing books.

Page 11 Answer Map

(Refer to any atlas or encyclopedia for California locations.)

Page 15 - Section 2: Quiz Time!

1. He lives in a summer cottage in Pacific Grove, in California's Central Coast. There is a lot of fog, golf courses, and shops near his house.
2. Mom couldn't look after the dog, and he gave Dad a body to talk to.
3. Bandit jumped into Dad's cab at a truck stop in Nevada and sat there.
4. He had a red bandanna around his neck instead of a collar.
5. He's a loner, he has to be cautious, nobody pays much attention to him.
6. He's the custodian. He's fair and doesn't look cross when he cleans.
7. When someone steals out of his lunch, little kids with runny noses, walking to school slow, and when his dad says "Keep your nose clean, kid."
8. He wishes somebody would stop stealing the good stuff out of his lunchbag and that Dad and Bandit would visit him and take him to school.
9. *The Great Lunchbag Mystery*
10. It's white with a brown bear in the middle.

Page 17 - Problem Solving: Think it Through

L.H.	G.S.	A.S.	A.S.	T.K.
S.S.	P.S.	S.F.	T.S.	E.S.

Page 19 - Section 3: Quiz Time!

1. It wasn't a good idea for a new boy in school to be a snitch.
2. He sent a call out over the CB radio for someone going to Pacific Grove.
3. Quilted down jacket with a lot of pockets & a hood that zips into the collar.
4. Go to the dentist, get some new shoes, went to Katy's for dinner.
5. He wrote a fictitious name (pseud) on his lunch bag.
6. Chili out of a can, frozen chicken pies.
7. A new book, Henshaw's *Beggar Bears.*
8. Mother bear who teaches her cubs to beg from tourists in Yellowstone, they wake up in the middle of winter hungry, a ranger takes care of them.
9. Lunch with a Famous Author and with winners from other schools.
10. His mom goes to her nursing class.
11. Lose some of their hearing in their left ear, get out of shape, get ulcers.

Page 22 - Section 4: Quiz Time!

1. When they are carrying too heavy a load.
2. Everybody seemed to know his dad who kidded around and played video games. Leigh stood up tall and ate steak, mashed potatoes with gravy.
3. "Find him and punch him in the nose."
4. Upset/Angry. His dad hadn't called, Bandit was gone, a boy was there.
5. He heard the boy's voice and didn't want to hear anymore.
6. He stays trapped in his room with the babies.
7. He was mad at his mom for divorcing his dad.
8. He didn't have to pretend anymore. He has learned to say what he thinks.
9. They got married too young, she was tired of life on the road, she grew up.
10. Everyone else has problems. "You gotta think positively."

Answer Key *(cont.)*

Page 25 Traveling Across the U.S.

1. 1,016 miles
2. 1,356 miles
3. 3,111 miles
4. 10.37 tanks
5. You would have to stop in Reno, between Reno and Denver, five times between Denver and St. Louis, between St. Louis and Cincinnati, between Cincinnati and Pittsburgh, and two times between Pittsburgh and New York.
6. $155.55
7. Answers will vary.

Page 26 - Feelings

1. angry
2. tired
3. friendly
4. sick
5. loving
6. hurting
7. strong
8. frightened
9. curious
10. shy
11. confused
12. peaceful

Page 27 - Section 5: Quiz Time!

1. It was quiet, like church. Brown sticks turned into thousands of orange and black butterflies. It was beautiful and made Leigh feel good!
2. Metal boxes that said "Alarm System."
3. Boys-monsters, lasers, creatures from outer space. Girls-horses or poems.
4. An apology about Bandit written on a napkin and $20.00.
5. Save it toward a typewriter.
6. Order of events: 5, 1, 2, 3, 4.
7. A beat-up black lunch box.
8. His alarm went off in the cafeteria.
9. The noise startled people, everyone in the cafeteria looked around, Mr. Fridley grinned, the principal came over. Leigh had to give a demonstration.

Page 32 - Buying Hardware Supplies

1. about $.30 or 30 cents
2. about $.60 or 60 cents
3. $9.21
4. Answers will vary
5. $16.56 / $3.44
6. (A) $.76 (B) $5.00 (C) $.59 or $.60
7. a battery clip > a disc magnet

Page 33 - Section 6: Quiz Time!

1. Ten-foot wax man, poem about butterflies, lunch box mystery, and finally he finished a description of trucking a load of grapes down Highway 152.
2. His sisters set it off on purpose. It was driving Barry's mom crazy.
3. Honorable Mention.
4. The teachers discovered the winning poem had been copied from a book.
5. He hadn't read her books.
6. He wrote honestly about something he knew and had strong feelings about. He made her really feel what it was like. He did not imitate.
7. If she wrote in pencil or on the typewriter, did she ever have books rejected, were her characters real people, and did she ever have pimples.
8. Did she ever meet Boyd Henshaw and "What's he like?". She had, and that he was a nice young man with a wicked twinkle in his eye.
9. He would have to go to school with him.
10. Leigh was proud of his burglar alarm. When his dad called, he changed "I'm fine" to "I'm great" as he thought of the success of his alarm.

Page 35 - Electricity Experiments

Insulators: eraser, plastic, wood, rock

Conductors: key, paper clip, metals

Page 37 - Parts of a Letter

1. A colon instead of a comma after the greeting.
2. Inside address (company's address)
3. Sincerely, Your's truly, Your friend, Best wishes, Cordially, etc.
4. Between the city and state, after the day, after the greeting, and after the closing.
5. Street, city, state, month, Dear, person's name, first word of the closing, the signature, and the beginning letter of each sentence.

Page 44 - Unit Test Answers

Matching: e, c, f, g, b, a, h, d **True/False:** All False.

Short Answer: 1. Mr. Fridley 2. Barry 3. Miss Martinez 4. Katy

Essay: Answers will vary.

Page 45 - Response Answers will vary. Accept any reasonable answer that students can support with reference to the book.